DARWIN'S MICROSCOPE

DARWIN'S MICROSCOPE

Kelley Swain

First published in Great Britain in 2009 by Flambard Press
Holy Jesus Hospital, City Road, Newcastle upon Tyne NE1 2AS
www.flambardpress.co.uk

Reprinted 2010

Typeset by BookType
Cover Design by Gainford Design Associates
Printed in Great Britain by Cpod, Trowbridge, Wiltshire

Front Cover Image: Radiolaria, SEM, Eye of Science/
Science Photo Library
Radiolaria. Coloured scanning electron micrograph (SEM) of the shells of various radiolaria. Radiolaria are single-celled protozoans that are found in marine plankton. They have a silicate skeleton with pores through which pseudopodia (false feet, not seen) of protoplasm project. As the animal floats in ocean currents the pseudopodia trap food particles on which the radiolarian feeds. Magnification: x150 when printed 10 centimetres wide.

A CIP catalogue record for this book is available from the British Library.
ISBN: 978-1-906601-03-4

Flambard Press wishes to thank Arts Council England
for its financial support.

Flambard Press is a member of Inpress.

The paper used for this book is FSC accredited.

Contents

Descent

Ex omnia conchis

Ex omnia conchis (all from shells): *Darwin family motto written by Charles's grandfather, Erasmus Darwin, based on Erasmus's own theory of species transmutation.*

'Sweet is the lore which Nature brings;
Our meddling intellect
Mis-shapes the beauteous forms of things: –
We murder to dissect.'

Wordsworth, from 'The Tables Turned'

Vestiges

Shadows in Chalk

at the White Cliffs of Dover

Silken outlines on a wall with scars and scrapes,
crystallised and hidden places.

Shadows leaning hard against a white cliff face
above a channel, splitting continents.

Silhouettes in sediment, of a hundred thousand years,
sea creatures crushed to dust, soaked with rain and blood.

Shapes unchanging only while the sun remains,
immortalised in chalk, lines we scrape and wipe away.

Darwin's Letter

Yellow-blossomed partridge-pea,
hard-thorned buffalo bur:

asking for these seeds
with his humble Victorian air,

Charles Darwin wrote a letter.
He had a wish to *experimentise*:

I have read with unusual interest
your very interesting paper . . .

on the flowers of 'Solanum rostratum' . . .
if you would send me some seeds . . .

Though the letter reached its mark,
nine days later, Darwin died.

Italic text from a letter by Darwin to J. Todd, 19 April 1882 (now in the University of Kansas Library).

Deprived of Its Medium

Hope is the thing with feathers
Bird in a bell jar
That perches in the soul,
suffocating –
and sings the tune without the words,
proves the ether
and never stops at all
runs out.

Italic text from 'Hope Is the Thing With Feathers' by Emily Dickinson.

Fossil Memories

. . . or, what is left of Darwin

What is left of a man
when two hundred years have passed,
his cousins distantly pleased
with their thin-running blood,
his face on a banknote,

his home a museum
where ten children played, where he fell ill
and roused himself to walks and work countless times,
where he loved his family but lost his faith,
where he hesitated and wondered and was spooked
into writing a book which changed our future
as well as our past.

See him wrapped in cold towels
shaking with fever, or turning from his daughter's
death-bed, knowing his wife's God
would be her only solace,
or turning from his son's death-bed,
never saying aloud how nature had selected against
this loved but deficient boy.

See him hunched at a wooden table,
one hundred barnacles systematically aligned,
his touchy stomach the worse for the alcohol-preservative smell,
his eyes squinted towards the creatures he came to hate.

Weathering of time,
rust of human memory,
snowflakes of a glacier,
pebbles of a mountain,
fist-sized rock of a whale's baleen,
little but a fossil of a man.

Down, Bromley

Black-eyed sheep
graze a February-flooded field.
Wood-pigeon, fat, suspended,
and red-breast singing –
singing over cold February stone.
Bright sharp sun in a blue sky
over couples of mallards –
sleek-headed sapphire Drake
or emerald – she chooses.
Glistening mud and green,
trying, hopeful,
in the certain spring.
Clumped cattails, a dredged canal –
and a church spire, always, distant.

Voyage

Morning Watch

As a hard-boiled sun
cracked the horizon near
arid Patagonia,
a strange mist settled on the ship.

Every drop of frosted glass lived,
each delicate dancing snowflake
a just-hatched spider,
their thousand bodies a web
of twinkling dew upon the deck.

One by one, the translucent drops
lifted ethereal lassos
to the wind, whose breath
ballooned them to parachute-flight
onto the sea, evaporating
the mist as silently as it had come.

Ship's Naturalist

It was futile, I decided,
to look for red tides.

The animalcules making them up
come and go with the currents:

for months our ship sailed
through clear waters.

One morning, roused by shouts
from the crew, I hurried on deck

to see red water surrounding us,
stretching as far as I could see,

grainy, orangey-red,
a swathe of rust-water.

The surface was broken
by buoyant bodies of dead fish;

seabirds wheeled overhead,
screaming, diving after them.

I scooped a jar of water,
held it, my hands trembling

with excitement, the water
trembling with life.

A droplet under my microscope
quivered with broken ruby snowflakes.

The next morning the sea was clear,
as if the red tide had never been.

Cetacean Introduction

The whale does not
exist to you,
in your small boat
with the water
an obsidian dance floor
for the birds you watch,
with the water
unbroken by creatures
you do not imagine
underneath,
does not
exist to you,
in your orange life-vest,
with notebook close-
gripped and binoculars
settled for looking
to the skies,
does not
exist to you
as the wind tugs
your hair, combing
it with salt and low-tide smell
from the mountains of shells
piled on the beach upwind.

So when the water changes,
when the birds yell
and lift off,
when you suddenly feel
small,
when the breath breaks
the surface
next to you
rocking your boat,
when you grip your
life-vest,
when your binoculars

fall and you stare
at the grey mountain
rising from the sea,
which rolls and rolls,
a barnacled stage,
marked and polished
and marked –

After the back thins
and rolls away
into a wide fin
with a mountain range
along its edge,
after it slips
below the gloss
sending ripples outward
to slide under your small boat,
after the birds return
and settle,
after puffs of wind
sweep the smooth
glassy footprint away,
after you loosen
your grip on the life-vest
and your boat stops
rocking,

you turn your gaze down

to look past
the obsidian glaze.

New Hand on Deck

Legs wobble,
stomach turns

like this cork
I bob on in the sea.

Ocean? It means awe.
Dread.

I am not even a speck
in this deadly element.

Why did I join the crew
of this damnable vessel?

The crew laughs as I puke
shellfish over the port side,

tells me I will
'find my sea legs soon.'

But fins, flippers,
not legs,

are what I need.
I will not 'find' them.

Glacier Blue

The glacier takes sun into itself.

Gathers the colours – red, orange, yellow, green –
collecting them into cold compression.

Thousands of years of ice compacting, squeezing out air –
it can collect the sun, breathlessly suck in the colours –
but one escapes.

Blue, glacier blue –
not blue like the sky or Caribbean seas,
not like the robin's egg or the silk iris petal –

glacier blue.

Quicker than red, orange, yellow, green –
these colors fall into the glacier and cannot turn back –

glacier blue shivers away in time to escape –

to glow from the ice
so it is the only colour we see.

Loss of a Whale

The giant carcass sinks
into the abyss, taking
barnacles on its belly,
suckerfish on its side,
tons of blubber, gallons of oil,
racks of baleen to fossilise
into small black rocks;
taking wails, clicks, echoes
that will sound no more
as the body sinks past the reach
of sunlight into the crushing dark,
past schools of porpoise,
past eight-legged giants, small beside it;
water rushes past the curving fluke,
fanned out, bending up
in a final flip; streams of bubbles
float to the surface, glimmer and pop
thousands of feet above, a chain
linking whitecaps to the deep fathoms.

First the giant sinks past nothing,
last breath pouring out,
pressure bending in a body
which has never travelled so deep;
now pulls heavily past wrecks
of humanity; great broken ships,
splintered masts,
the arching figurehead
of a lady's bust,
hair and breasts covered
with green slime,
her companions empty skulls,
skittering silent creatures,
her blind eyes watching the carcass
float down in the pitch,
lit only by phosphorescent pulses
of pigment-less life,

every pulse of the creatures
revealing organs built to withstand
the smothering dark, the sea floor.

The whale slowly touches,
delicately crushes rock,
blind glowing creatures,
comes to rest
where undersea vents
provide an oasis
of nutrient heat in the freezing dark,
bubbling up red life
where no sunlight
is needed or ever seen;
the body stretches, metres long,
into the dark, while hagfish,
ancient slimy creatures
wriggling along the ocean floor,
feed solely on whale remains.

Submersible Captain

A small metal
placenta,

protecting me from all
my body cannot withstand:

darkness, water pressure,
lack of oxygen.

Remote gears whirr, buzz;
I descend, slowly.

Powerful lamp a spark
in the Black Forest,

the beam reaches –
I search for the wreck,

relic of war,
submarine,

find a different relic
on the uneven floor.

Whale bones glint
into view;

Not white, no sun
to bleach them,

great grey ribs
bend into darkness.

The vessel settles
into mechanical twilight.

I am the first, the only,
to kneel at this grave.

Bones

Bones in the rock
in the ice
in the dirt
in the water.

An island made of bones.

A planet made of bones,
bones of ancestors
fallen from wars,
        from predators
        from disease,

fallen
from never having stood.

Bones sinking
        into mud
        into earth
        into lava
into sea floor,

bones compressed
        to chalk
        to coal

        which we use to heat our bones.

The Unsettling of Dunes

First we run our feet through silken sediment,
undulating dunes plucked particle
after particle by fingers of wind.

Then we feel the muffled crunch
of calcium carbonate layers beneath
from chalk of ivory sand dollar,
crumpled keel of pelican, dust of reptile,
scale of fish, shell of oyster,
to sift through our fingers, and *sedimentum.*

Ooids compress with the weight of sand,
of in-seeping water,
laminae after laminae coming to rest
one on another until they fuse,
and coquina along the shore
hold mosaic shells until waves abrade
and they crumble, *sedimentum*,
to be curled from beach to sea,
to be sifted, floated, carried,
to be filtered by fish, pelicans, oysters,
sand dollars, and again,
sedimentum.

Tectonic Motion

We chart it, draw it,
connect its dots,
measure, compile,
assess, organise.

We embrace it, deny it,
think nothing of it, but it is there,

churning itself through rain,
heat, earthquakes, volcanoes;
through tectonic plates grinding
almost too slow to measure;
through ghosts of icebergs
leaving boulders and grooves behind.

Slow time. Not our time.

We see drastic changes wrought by
time slower than we will ever comprehend,
slower than all the generations of our families,
slower than the time before our ancestors
had legs, or were naked, or stood.

Time slower than before anything lived on land,
time slower than before anything lived.

It is neither there for us,
nor against us. It is there.

It will be there long after charts, diagrams,
pictures, specimens, books have evaporated
to dust, disappearing with the wind, ground back
into the great mortar of molecules of Earth,
and no one will exist to call it 'Earth'.

There will be no one to remember,
no one to forget, no one watching,
and it will still carry on.

Bird Island, Baja

Thrust of foot, flush of feather –
I hold my breath; they walk on water.

Cormorant, pelican, a dark stampede
of hollow bones rattles around me.
An acrid beach, living sand
where black stains white,
spills to bay. The moving island, lifting.
Necks strain against gravity.

Hundreds of wings pump a heartbeat on water.

I am an eye in this storm, this rushing
whispering roar of foot and feather.

Reverse Cartography

Those tiny worms in sea mud
are your truly ancient ancestors,
and is it bad?

They are before bad, good, gross;
before Adam and Eve,
before legs, brains, eyes.

Before feeling,
before thinking,
before words,
before six thousand years ago,

before alive things left the seas,
before alive things returned to the seas,
before alive things left the seas again.

The magnet of north switches with south,
continents crash, pull apart,
ice coats, melts, re-coats land,
tides rise, fall, rise again,
heat bubbles from inside,

and the churning pressure-cooker
outside the crust, the most animated
of inanimate forces, determines what persists
on a map only chartable in reverse.

Eulogy for a Cephalopod

1

Dark myth,
Giant Terror –
suckers, tearing arms,
razor beak:
The Kraken pulls ships
to the crushing Deep.

As a child I stand tiptoe,
nose pressed to cool glass
filled with twilight water,
peering into blue depths,
searching for The Monster.

It does not appear.

2

Years later, peering again
through glass into dim blue,
I see the octopus in full bloom.

The billowing parachute
breathes water;
see-through skin
and glass-kissing suckers
putty-stretch in every direction,
whisk the water, stirring
a whirlpool of pigment-stained flesh
which dances over rock and plant,
rusty orange and brown
in the twilight water.

The eye –
yellow, round, large,
sees me.

3

The surf is too heavy
to wade deeper than our feet,
but sand-coated relics
cross-stitch the high-tide line.

We peer, and wonder:
'What is it?'
'An octopus.'
'Is it dead?'
'Don't touch it.'

Noodle-tangled arms,
plum-sized head.
It is round, translucent,
and as we crouch
the centre swirls
and pulses with blue.

'It's alive.'

I take an abalone shell
from my pile
of beach-combed treasures,
gently scoop the octopus
so it rests
for a moment
in the iridescent moon.

Towards Perfection

Long, slow, unplanned precision:
deceptive perfection, this spiny scallop,
glossy purple-and-white,
the whorl incrementally widening
with each smooth ridge.

Read a simple fortune
in its parallel-lined palm:
the lifeline is the outer edge,
where the throwing over
of each new layer ceased.

Protection grown, accident
enhancing standard armour.
Brittle-plated fish-defying bivalve,
sharply outstretching
vaulted pink-and-brown cousins.

Invaded by a symmetrical hole
drilled precisely beside the spines
where another mollusc reached in,
dissolving the soft flesh,
or a small octopus embraced the shell,
using its only sharp part –
its beak – to scrape persistently,
grinding each layer away, stretching in
a thin arm, grasping the flesh,
leaving the shell hollow,
the unplanned sculpture drifting,
polished by tongues of waves.

Origins

What the Toad Said

The botanist
said there was no toad
in the greenhouse,
but we had heard him
belching through
the fog and dew
of the locked room
where mist whispered
through heavy air
onto ginko,
liverwort,
Queen Anne's lace,
onto the far wall of rock
covered with hanging ferns,
soft moss, and mould,
the room where flecks of dust
transmuted into prisms
as they drifted
into creamy sunlight
streaking through pollen-
dusted windows,
the room where we closed the door
to breathe
the reciprocal breath
of *flora, flora, everywhere.*

In the Lab

1. *Survey*

Embryos of chicken and pig,
necks folded at obtuse angles,
yellow in jars. Humming
vent swallows fumes; cool
musk permeates, mixes
with mothball, formalin, dust.

Jaws, scales, fur, and feathers,
all stiffened. Iridescent shingles
on purple Lepidoptera.
Trilobite fossils from Utah,
thumbnail-sized.

Parrot, eagle, old penguin
crusty with dandruff.
Wood duck wire-stiffened
into permanent flight.
Empty, peeling box-tortoise shell.
Snakes spiraled into glass
with faded labels, withered egg-cases.
Eyeless snapping turtles,
rusty-pink, rotting, stuffed, tagged,
boxed, jarred, examined.

2. *Gastropoda*

Endangered Queen: pale conch,
dethroned, sitting heavy on a shelf.
Slow-stretching foot, snail-creature,
leaked this crown into hard existence
under crush of salt water.

Linear development? Tiny spiral at first,
whorling continuously outward, around.

3. *Echinodermata*

Tangled woven basket-star
lashed across the ocean floor,
arms of rope now dried
brittle and hard.

Sand dollars, in childhood,
were pirate gold,
now they are animals
related to sea urchins:
brittle shell, five-lobed stamp
filtering microscopic food:
dried in boxes, broken
filters leak sand.

4. *Arthropoda*

Plastic dish, dried insects:
a huge, swept-off
window ledge.
Sharp, spiny, mean, brittle wings,
trick-of-my-eye movements –
they *are* dead –
as I turn the dish.

Did this cicada
mate before it died?
Sap-suckling from roots
for seventeen years
dark underground
to end in a mad burst:
mating, starvation, death.
Four days of sunlight,
of humming flight.

A cube of plastic
suspends a barnacle.
Darwin studied cirripeds
for over six years.
Strange creatures, upside-down
in their housing, legs propelling
food in and down to the mouth,
tiny volcano erupting
strands of flesh.
I leave this curl-footed crustacean
within six minutes.

5. *Reptilia*

Sea turtle skeleton –
my mind adds flesh and colour
until it swims in Caribbean waters,
sharp-beaked stab crunching a shell,
sending clouds of sand
into shallow swells.

Hellbender salamander –
North American giant,
elusive occupant
of the Appalachian Trail –
now occupant of this jar,
belly slit, wrinkled, crummy,
rusty red, eyes folded
into skin above a wide-seamed mouth.
It waggled with a belly-dragging gait,
flat tongue flicking out.

6. *Aves*

Wooden board, pegged-down legs:
nine, each different, not paired,

claws curved, gripping wood,
a scaly leg ending in air,

an entire body amputated –
stumps that stop, dusty glue and cobwebs,

hawk foot –
mouse trembling, claws grasping –

duck foot –
paddling through pond weeds –

sparrow foot –
rustling delicate branches, seeds.

7. *Mammalia, monotremata*

The platypus, two feet long,
tip of beak to end of tail,
head taxidermied upwards,
squints, smiles, beak line curving up,
fur thick, insulating,
rubbery beak dried hard in death.

Alive, the sensitive beak
sees electricity;
the platypus hunts underwater,
eyes tightly closed,
looking for pulses –
crayfish heartbeats,
skittering insect larvae –
food can stay still,
but it can't switch off.

Blind, eyes covered
with a pink skin layer,
young platypus squirm
in deep dark, safe and blue
with heat from mother
who squeezes out thick cream
to pool in her fur.

Once called 'paradoxus',
it was thought a hoax,
the specimens were searched
for stitches attaching duck-like beak
to beaver-like body.
But it lives, even now, in Australia,
rummaging leaves in streambeds,
snatching edibles, head swishing
back and forth, eyes squeezed shut,
feeling rocks, logs, leaves,
drawing maps of riverbeds.

8. *Mammalia, Homo sapiens*

Shells, jars, humming silence.

I respirate in this room
of expired respiration.

The eurypterid,
pale swathes on stone,
hunted the seas
millions of years ago,
left an impression.

Particles the heron inhaled
in life were particles
the eurypterid excreted,
particles that evaporated,
that rained, that I now inhale
with each inspiration.

Illumination of an Empty Room

I hold the pink fetus
of the kitten
on my blue latex-gloved hand.

I stare at the tiny dead thing,
crescent-shaped and naked, with beginnings,
minute forms, of arms, ears –
small, dark, unopened eyes.

We cut open the mother,
her uterine tube
thickly lumped with a litter of six,
each ball packed with blood vessels.
We felt around the clotted walls
to pull out the frozen life on a string.

Now, in the sterile room,
cloaked in heavy formaldehyde
that sticks in the back of my throat
so every breath tastes of death –

here, holding the stiff, heavy cat in the sink,
rinsing out her viscera,
brown blood flowing
into steel wash basin;

after the crunch of cutting open
the ribs with scissors,
pushing fibrous muscle to the side –

here and now I believe
in Science, and Death.

I hold the cashew embryo,
feel the weightlessness
on the pad of my little finger,
stroke its tiny, soft, pink-skinned head.

I am full of empty understanding,
numb, choking, with grit
of chemical fumes in my hair;
alone, a poet in a room full of scientists.

Later, the hottest shower I can stand
washes the smell away.
Still, with every breath – I taste it,
and wonder what the chemicals I breathe
preserve in me.

A Smoke at Dusk

The night we sat outside
on a warm autumn evening,
friends, roommates,
you taught me how to puff
and taste without choking,
two twenty-year-old girls
sitting on a porch
in white rocking chairs,
smoking cigars
like two old men.

I thought the sky was filled
with bats, small pointed shapes
flitting, diving, flowing in flocks
over rooftops, darting
through the evening air,
but they were chimney swifts,
swarming to their brick abodes
at dusk, flocking to sleep,
riding in waves of pointed clouds,
twenty and more birds,
beyond the warm clouds
of cigar smoke.

The Smells of Good Death and Bad Death

We know why we can't stand
the smell of dead flesh.

My hair smells
like liquid chemicals
filling skinless dead cats
we scrape in lab,
their still-furred faces
twisted into squinched eyes,
their stiff tongues jutting past fangs.
This one was a Siamese,
this one a tabby,
you can tell how fat it was
by how many yellow globs
need cutting to see muscle striation:
pectoralis major, minor.

This cat under my scalpel –
too big for the shiny silver tray,
furred paw dripping preservative
onto the tabletop – this cat is here
because someone did not take him home,
while my cat, ancient, black-and-white,
mean as hell, is not dripping on the lab table
under the wrinkle-nosed gazes
of safety-goggled students,
because we kept her, even when Mom said no.
This cat, the dead one, stiff and pumped with fluid,
smells like inquiry and plastic bags,
science and mass-gassed death,
the dead-end of evolving genes.

*

But losing its last oomph of green,
the gingko leaf smells like moist earth
and autumn, like hibernation;
it feels like silk and rubber,
a wide fan with mountain peaks
rolling smoothly along its edge,
ridged veins, a sunburst of parallel lines,
leaf-braille: *this is gingko*, my fingers say.

We toss great handfuls of yellow
gingko leaves into the air, at each other;
they rain into the back of my shirt, stick in my hair.
The tree has exploded its gold
upon the red-brick sidewalk; we scoop and whisk
handfuls and handfuls of the green-gold medallions
at each other, never too old to play.

And why do we love the smell of fall,
of thousands of leaves, dying and dead?

A Fall Evening

Standing at the pond's edge
I think of Ophelia,
of letting sleep take over,
returning to the womb.

The numb sea
reclaims countless children
and all ponds run to the ocean.
What is one more child?

I want to take the flowers from you,
your way of saying 'I'm sorry',
and put them in my hair,
dance into the water, but

we no longer know what kind
of flowers they are.
We have forgotten
what they mean.

Lovely Mollusc

Upon my collarbone
rests half a bivalve
no bigger than my thumbnail,
smooth, white.

From a beach of shells
in Northern Ireland
I selected this one,
with a perfect tiny hole
at the top; put a blue string
through it, better than any necklace
I could have bought.

A tiny creature used to live inside
with muscles, gills, blood, mouth –
all tossed and tumbled ashore
where, after days, or months, or years
I happened to pick it
from a thousand other shells.

What little bivalve
is better remembered
not just for the nacreous layer,
smooth, white, but for the tiny
animal once living within?

Feeding the Corn Snake

Flicking her red switch of tongue, searching
for the thawed mice, black and glistening,
she unhinges her orange jaw in the hot red light.

Her eyes glow transparent pink
under the heat lamp as she turns,
metallic, wicked, ancestral,
to look at me through the glass.
Of course Eve was tempted.

She shed her first skin yesterday. It drapes
on the table, a pale trophy.

Taking a mouse head first, she plunges, mouth wide,
into its wet fur, its feet folding back as her muscles
ripple it in. A bead of blood rolls down
her belly, matching her scales.

Soon only the tail is left, but the light
shines through her, and I see the dark bulge sliding
to her thicker parts until it smoothes and is gone;
she lifts herself, turns her head, looks for more.

The Ninth Commandment

It wasn't the watching –
a film of chimps, a gang of them, hunting
a Colobus monkey. It wasn't the suspense
of the chase, blockers cutting off escape
routes, alpha male moving in, making
the kill. It wasn't the screaming fear
of the prey or the screaming excitement
of the predators, on-looking female chimps
on the ground, babies clutched to their bellies,
while the males scaled the trees
to surround the chosen one.

It was the false witness borne,
resonating in long-dead
jeers and rotten fruit thrown
at neighbors twitching on a spike,
or a spit, or the gallows, or a tree branch –

trembling through excitement
in even the narrator's voice,
and in me, seeing myself up there
in those trees, canines gleaming
warm with marrow and flesh.

Thermodynamics of Immortality

When I die, scatter my ashes to the wind to settle
on a forest floor where earthworms buffet

through rich humus, where I pass from intestines
as nutrients taken by acorns, sprout, stretch

toward sunlight, year after year, inch my way to a branch
steeped with cicada eggs so I fall to the ground

and burrow, eat sap for seventeen years,
burst forth for two frenzied days seeking a mate,

when a burnt-ember cardinal snatches me, red
and cackling, catching warm air pockets from the pavement

until winter moves in; I huddle on a branch, fall asleep,
thud to the cold ground, dissolve slowly

into the icy creek, flow like mercury,
weave over stones around roots under branches, turn warm,

briny, pull into a spiny starfish, pump
into slow feet, and crawl again.

Descent

Pure Admiration

In the belly of the cave
where perfect dark hangs its cloak,
where gossamer threads drape over stone,
where great pinnacles clear as ice grow
by trickle and drip of mineral
carried by water through miles
of jigsaw cracks,

they come, wriggling
through water-widened crevasses,
guttural sounds echoing in the slick
cathedral halls of stone;
they come, sliding, grasping,
sloshing and rustling through water
still winding through the solid,
the changing, rock.

With thick insulating skins, ropy
appendages, waterlogged feet,
waists cinched metallic,
heavy, hard protection
at their heads. With lamps.
They are the first and only
to admire the rock.

The instant the beam hits,
the crystals begin to turn, slowly,
opaque white, muddied
at the first soft touch of light.

Mating of the Silkworm Moth

His quill-feather antennae twitch
with her effervesce of a single particle,

inscribing a message onto his nerves,
launching him into the velvet dark

where he follows barely perceptible
breadcrumbs of chemical breath,

tracing her perfume until it thickens
in the ink of night, until she

permeates his senses, her pheromones
swelling in the air, solidifying

into herself, there, on a leaf
in the dark, where he finds her.

The Lake District

Sometimes we come upon a carcass.
Once I found a ram's skull,
rippling horns curving away
from huge holes once filled with eyes.
Once, just a sweep of wool,
dirty, bloodied, smeared across the grass
and into mud. I wondered
what predators hid in these steep hills –
Sheepdogs gone bad?
Large birds, beaked to sever vertebrae
at the base of the skull?
What predators other than gravity?

We walk in springtime
when mothers call:
A low, gravelly BAA from the ewes – stay close.
A high-pitched *baa!* from the lambs, who stumble,
blinded beneath the thick fern cover of hillsides.
We hear panic in both voices
until they find each other and fall quiet.

Sometimes we hear a little one call,
call, and call,
and we follow the winding trail
beaten out by thin hooves over seasons,
stop for a drink of water,
fix a shoelace, crest the hill,
and still we hear it calling.

Plumed Magician

We think we spy
through binocular
lenses,

but this small
white-and-brown
plumed falcon
sits in high treetops,
ignoring us,

escaping us.

*

How many days
do we walk,
searching the leaves
for her dart-shaped
shadow, while

she watches
a thread
on my coat
unravel.

*

Today in the park
we glimpse her

flitting from bare
white birch bark
to dense cluster
of green pine.

Then our Merlin
simply disappears.

Fallen Armour

When my friend's brain burst a small secret
called aneurism, killing him,
I was glad he was not an only child.

We had two children, Mom said,
to replace your dad and me but not add
to the brimming human population.

After I was born, Dad got 'fixed'.
Later, happy to see Daddy home,
my brother took a running leap into his lap.

*

With sea turtles, odds are stacked
in favour of survival only if the mother
successfully buries her clutch,

if no ants attack a just-hatched egg,
leaving a sunken leathery shell
and tiny skeleton inside,

if rooting pigs don't crush
the buried nest, nosing
the sand for a hatchling meal,

if poachers don't dig up the nest,
place the eggs in a bucket
to sell at cheap bars for false virility,

if a hatchling wins the race
to the sea, missed by gull,
crab, fish, or eel,

if she completes the weeks-long
marathon to a swirling nursery of Sargasso
weed, a current pulling her since birth,

if she survives there for twenty years,
ventures into the open sea,
mates,

if she makes it back to her beach
and it is unobstructed by jetty,
still free of asphalt.

*

But there, poachers take her,
flip her on her back so she can only flap,
collect her newly-laid eggs,

rip off her shell.
It ends up here, bleaching
under a Mexican sun,

jig-sawed into puzzle pieces
which lock and sprout from the spine,
flatten, fuse into an oval,

while over and around, herbs
sprout from the shell,
grow pale green nerve cords,

veins, arteries of sage,
which some cultures use for prayer,
which I burned at my father's grave.

The Katydid Chorus

The katydid chorus rises,
metallic hum, answering, joining,
one by one until even the hum
of the plane above cannot be heard.

Safety in numbers:
when the katydid-hunter
strikes, the unfortunate victim
will be paralysed,

a frozen snack for larvae to eat,
day by day, still fresh meat
until it expires: but the chorus
sounds no quieter.

We are connected,
for the katydid has made it as far,
and we share a spot
on its branch of time.

Monarch Sunset

One night in August the trees burn November.

The lighthouse spins its cyclops eye to the Atlantic.
The full moon rises ivory in the purple sky,
the sun tilts low on the horizon, sends
its swathe of light simmering across the bay.

But the conflagration is on the peninsula's trees:
hundreds of monarchs pairing tip to tip,
flecked with dying day,
melting green leaves with copper,
blazing with slow thermal radiance,
pausing on these trees, for this hour,
to gather and merge in flame.

Spherical Motion

There is movement in this sphere,
of millimetre-
measured subduction,
oceanic trenches widening,
sulphurous vents
bubbling gaseous fumes,
mountain ranges pushing above
the sea-line after earthquakes,
pulling calcium shells inland
to harden in the desert sun,
dry-cracking mud flats
stripped of water,
oxygen-silicon tetrahedra
crystallizing halite, quartz, talc,
coral reefs stacking pinhead
houses one upon another,
octagon-columned pathways
torn asunder,
edging the base of one country
and the tip of its neighbour,
magma pockets rising from deep
layers of rock,
bulging into batholiths, wrenching
into canyons –
four-and-a-half-billion years of rock
birthing and swallowing itself
in an unceasing groan.

There is movement on this sphere,
of floss-
spinning arthropods,
ungulate toes widening,
methane-venting fauna
leaking green fumes,
naked mole rats pushing soil
in blind trembling lines,
pulling roots to gnaw
with translucent teeth,
cackling shore birds
dancing across water,
chlorophyll in bud and leaf
sculpting stamen, pistil, petal
from sunlight, gold dusted
upon fuzz-legged bees
packing pollen into stacked
octagons of wax,
microscopic creatures
sucking tidbits within moss,
giant leather-backed reptiles
rising from deep ocean trenches,
bursting to the surface, wrenching
into air –
one-hundred-fifty years or less
will see each birthed and swallowed
in the unceasing groan.

Acknowledgements

I would like to thank my mother, Kathy, for her unconditional love and support; my supervisors at Randolph-Macon Woman's College, particularly Doug Shedd (Biology), Laura-Gray Street and Jim Peterson (Creative Writing), Karin Warren (Environmental Studies), and Heidi Kunz (Literature), for their diverse contributions; and my Quill Drivers, for their inspiration.